War and Conflict in the Middle East™

Israel's War of Independence

Chris Hayhurst

The Rosen Publishing Group, Inc., New York

Published in 2004 by The Rosen Publishing Group, Inc.
29 East 21st Street, New York, NY 10010

Library of Congress Cataloging-in-Publication Data

Hayhurst, Chris.
Israel's war of independence / by Chris Hayhurst.
     p. cm. — (War and conflict in the Middle East)
Summary: Examines the history behind Israel's mid-twentieth
century battle for independence amid the surrounding Arab
nations, plus biographical notes on important figures and a look
at the effects of this war.
Includes bibliographical references and index.
ISBN 0-8239-4548-0 (library binding)
1. Arab-Israeli conflict—Juvenile literature. 2. Palestine—History—20th
century—Juvenile literature. 3. Israel—History—20th century—Juvenile
literature. [1. Arab-Israeli conflict—1948–1967. 2. Palestine—History—
20th century. 3. Israel—History—20th century.] I. Title. II. Series.
DS119.7.H3845 2003
956.04'2—dc21

                                                        2003009607

Manufactured in the United States of America

CONTENTS

INTRODUCTION 4

CHAPTER 1 HISTORICAL CLAIMS
TO PALESTINE 8

CHAPTER 2 A CALL TO ARMS 24

CHAPTER 3 THE ARAB INVASION 40

CHAPTER 3 AFTER THE WAR:
PROGRESS AND PROBLEMS 50

GLOSSARY 57

FOR MORE INFORMATION 59

FOR FURTHER READING 60

BIBLIOGRAPHY 61

INDEX 62

Open any major newspaper and you're bound to see headlines describing violence, death, and destruction. They come from all over the world—Colombia, Ireland, Chechnya, even the United States. But look a little closer. You might also notice that something else stands out: the region called the Middle East. It is home to countries like Israel, Iraq, Lebanon, and Iran. Many of those articles on violence come from this land. The Middle East is a place of incredible desert beauty. It is also a place where hatred and conflict between people are thousands of years old. Here are two headlines and their opening paragraphs, printed just days apart in the *New York Times*. The first story appeared on February 15, 2003. The second was printed on February 19.

Four Israelis Killed When Bomb Destroys Tank
Jerusalem, Feb 15—Four Israeli soldiers were killed

today when a bomb planted by Palestinian militants destroyed a tank near an Israeli settlement in the northern Gaza Strip, the Israeli Army said. . .

Battle in Gaza City Kills 11 Palestinians
Gaza City, Gaza Strip (AP)—Israeli tanks and soldiers battled Palestinian militants in the streets of Gaza City before dawn Wednesday in violence that left 11 Palestinians dead, including a suicide bomber who tried to blow up a tank, Palestinians said. . .

Fighting between Palestinians and Israelis is at the heart of Middle Eastern problems. The Palestinians say they are fighting Israel to get back land that Israelis stole from them. Israel claims it is fighting terrorists who want only the destruction of Israel.

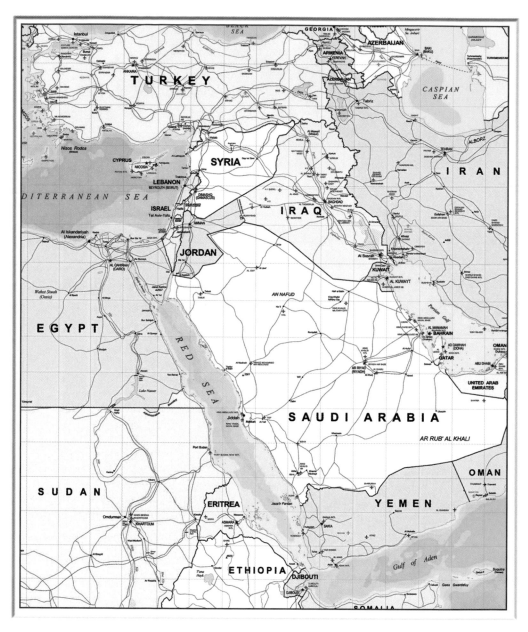

The Middle East is a large span of lands saddling western Asia and northeastern Africa across the Red Sea. It gets its name from its intersection between the West (Africa and Europe) and the East (Asia).

How the Palestinians lost their land to Israel and how Israel became a country are the focus of this book. A war between Israelis, Palestinians, and the rest of the Arab Middle East was triggered in the spring of 1948 by, among other things, Israel's declaration of independence. This was the moment Israel officially was recognized as an independent country. This war, known to Israelis as the War of Independence and to Palestinians as Al-Nakba, or "the Catastrophe," set into motion more than fifty years of violence and conflict. Today, as you can see by the articles on the preceding pages, that conflict continues.

CHAPTER 1

HISTORICAL CLAIMS TO PALESTINE

Israel today is the world's only "Jewish" country. That's not to say that Jews do not live anywhere else in the world. They do. In fact, Jews live everywhere. But Israel was established as a spiritual homeland for the Jewish people. It has become a place where Jews from anywhere in the world can come and settle. Today, the Israeli population includes immigrants from dozens of countries across the world.

But Israel is an island. It is not an island in the literal sense, for it is not surrounded by water. Instead it is an island because it is surrounded by countries that are nothing like itself. Israel is the only Jewish country in the sea of Arab and Islamic countries that make up the rest of the Middle East.

Today millions of people call Israel home, including Palestinians, other Arabs, Muslims, and Christians. They live in Israel and work in Israel, but there's a problem. Israel and its surrounding neighbors are in disagreement. They disagree on practically everything, including Israel's very right to exist.

To Israel's neighbors, Israel is part of a larger region known as Palestine. Historically, Palestine is a region east of the Mediterranean Sea. Palestine historically included parts of present-day Israel, Jordan,

The Dome of the Rock is one of the holiest places to Muslims worldwide. It sits in East Jerusalem, which is populated mostly by Muslims but is officially under Israeli rule.

and Egypt. To Jews—who make up the majority of the Israeli population—it's an area they believe was promised them by God in the Bible. To Muslims in the area, it has also been their homeland since ancient times. These Arab Muslims— the Palestinians—are outraged that the Jews, or Israelis, have made much of Palestine their home. They are outraged that today Palestinians don't have a home country of their own.

Today the Palestinians are limited to just two parts of Palestine: the West Bank, located between Israel and Jordan, and the Gaza Strip, a narrow length of land bordered by both Israel and Egypt. They're outraged that they've lost their ancient land to Israel. And they want it back.

Back to the Beginning: Claiming Territory in the Holy Lands

Israel's War of Independence is the product of history. To see how Israelis came to occupy what today is Israel, it's necessary to first take a trip far back in time.

It all began thousands of years ago with a people known as the Israelites. The Israelites came from Egypt, in northern Africa. They followed a man named Moses (a historical and biblical figure) out of Egypt and traveled north through the desert on foot until they came to what they knew as the Promised Land. They believed God had granted this land to them. The Israelites arrived at the Promised Land and conquered the people who lived there. They took over the region, called it Israel, and made their homes there, establishing the city of Jerusalem as the capital.

Israel Statistics

Total area: 8,019 square miles (20,770 square kilometers), slightly smaller than New Jersey
Border countries and territories: Egypt, Gaza Strip, Jordan, Lebanon, Syria, West Bank
Population: 6,029,529
Ethnicity: Jewish 80.1 %; non-Jewish, mostly Arab 19.9 %
Religion: Jewish 80.1 %, Muslim 14.6 %, Christian 2.1 %, other 3.2 %
Languages: Hebrew, Arabic, English
Capital: Jerusalem

West Bank Statistics

Location: West of Jordan
Total area: 2,263 square miles (5,860 sq km), slightly smaller than Delaware
Border countries: Israel, Jordan
Population: 2,163,667 (not including 182,000 Israeli settlers)
Ethnicity: Palestinian Arab 83 %, Jewish 17 %
Religion: Muslim 75 %, Jewish 17 %, Christian and other 8 %
Languages: Arabic, Hebrew, English

Gaza Strip Statistics

Location: Between Israel and Egypt on the Mediterranean Sea
Total area: 139 square miles (360 sq km), about twice the size of Washington, D.C.
Border countries: Egypt, Israel
Population: 1,225,911 (not including approximately 7,000 Israeli settlers)
Ethnicity: Palestinian Arab and other 99.4 %, Jewish 0.6 %
Religion: Muslim 98.7 %, Christian 0.7 %, Jewish 0.6 %
Languages: Arabic, Hebrew, English

Source: U.S. Central Intelligence Agency, *The World Factbook 2002*

Over the years, the Israelites established a connection with the region based not only on the land, but also on religion—the Jewish religion. King Solomon, who ruled nearly 1,000 years before the birth of Christ (4 BC), built a religious temple. The Temple, as it was known, became the center of the Jewish state. The Temple was a symbol with religious and national meaning. Even today this land is religiously the most important historic area to the Jews.

This painting, *Construction of the Temple of Jerusalem*, was painted by the Italian artist Pesellino in 1445.

Things went well for the Israelites for hundreds of years. Then, in 586 BC, the Babylonians (from present-day Iraq) attacked the Israelites. The Babylonians overwhelmed the Jewish defenders and destroyed the Temple. The Babylonians sent most of the Israelites into exile, forcing them to leave their homes and flee into the surrounding desert.

This type of conquest and exile is common to human history. The land of Israel was no exception. Over time, the Jews found themselves back in Jerusalem and the Promised Land. They rebuilt the Temple and then saw it destroyed again as new rulers swept in, were overthrown, and were swept out. Then, in AD 135, because of a bloody revolt, Jerusalem was completely destroyed. The Jews lost control over the area and were once again sent out into the surrounding desert (and, this time, to distant lands) to find new homes. This exile became known as the Diaspora.

Despite the Diaspora, the Jewish people never lost sight of their connection to the Holy Land. Some even stayed, hiding their religious practices. Others drifted back after only a few decades. Most, though, left and settled elsewhere. Even so, they vowed to someday return to live in their spiritual homeland.

Arab Rule Takes Over

Meanwhile, as the Jews established new homes elsewhere, the region east of the Mediterranean Sea came under the control of a people known as the Arabs in AD 638. The Arabs were from the vast desert land of Arabia, in southwest Asia. They had been expanding their empire throughout Asia and the Middle East. Their conquered territory came to include parts of three different continents (Asia, Europe, and Africa). This region ran from the Atlantic Ocean in the west to the Chinese border in the east.

With this dominance, the Arabs' main religion, Islam, became fundamental to the region. Arabic, their language, also came to dominate the peoples in those lands. Once established, Arabic and the religion of Islam stayed for good. This happened despite the fact that Arab rule in the area would be relatively short. They ruled the Middle East for a little longer than a century before being overthrown by other conquerors, who, in turn—one after another—were themselves conquered.

Finally, in the early sixteenth century, the land fell under the rule of the Ottoman Turks. The Turks would stay in power until the end of World War I (1914–1918).

Even as the Ottoman Turks ruled the area, Jews and Arabs continued to live there. Arabs continued to practice Islam. Jews practiced Judaism. Many Jews who had been sent into exile now found ways to return. As a result, even though the region was ruled by so-called outsiders, the Jewish people managed to remain connected to the area and continue the traditions of Jewish life.

Zionism and the Balfour Declaration

Since ancient times, the Jews of the biblical Diaspora believed they would one day be able to return to the

Promised Land. They thought it was only a matter of time before God would lead them back to their spiritual homeland. This religious belief was known as Zionism. They called the land Zion.

By the late nineteenth century, Zionism evolved from this strictly religious belief into a political movement to create a Jewish nation. Jews from around the world began speaking of a Jewish state. They talked openly of a place where Jews could once again live together, share their spirituality, and govern themselves. Of course, the land they spoke of was the Holy Land, known variously in ancient times as Judaea and Palestine.

The leader of the Zionist movement was a man named Theodor Herzl (1860–1904). Herzl saw that Jews across the world had been persecuted for their beliefs for more than 1,000 years. He looked at Europe and saw that more and more Jews were being discriminated against. He decided it was time for the Jewish people to do something about this oppression. He called for the first meeting of the World Zionist Congress, a group that would represent all Jews, their communities, and their organizations. That meeting was held on August 23, 1897, in Basel, Switzerland.

The first meeting of the World Zionist Congress included representatives of Zionist organizations from all over the world. Theodor Herzl was at the center of the action. Finally, after working for years on his own to advance the cause of Zionism, he was in charge of a central body that united all Zionist groups under one

Hungarian Theodor Herzl, pictured here, was a writer, playwright, and journalist. Herzl went on to lead the Zionist movement in the nineteenth century. He set up the first World Zionist Congress in 1897 to address the issue of anti-Semitism in Europe.

name. From this point on, the Zionists' voices would be heard loud and clear.

At the congress, Herzl and other Zionist leaders formulated their goals. The main priority would be the establishment of a national homeland for the Jewish people. Plans were made to settle the land of Israel. The Zionists did not know it then, but it would be more than fifty years before their dreams would finally come true with the establishment of the State of Israel.

The result of that first meeting of the World Zionist Congress was the creation of the World Zionist Organization (WZO). The WZO's official goal was to make a national home for the Jewish people in Palestine. Twenty years later, the achievement of that goal was finally in sight. During World War I, the British government controlled much of the Middle East, including Palestine. The Ottoman Turks were now out of control for good. On November 2, 1917, with the end of World War I near, the British government issued the Balfour Declaration.

For Zionist leaders like David Ben-Gurion and Chaim Weizmann, the Balfour Declaration was clear. The British would do everything they could to make a Jewish home in Palestine a reality. In addition, the Palestinians already living there would be treated well, and their rights would be honored.

To Ben-Gurion, the future prime minister of Israel, this was great news. He had worked hard through a group called the Jewish Legion for Britain to get to this point. Now his hard work had paid off. Chaim Weizmann had put in an

The Balfour Declaration

November 2, 1917

His Majesty's Government views with favor the establishment in Palestine of a national home for the Jewish people, and will use their best endeavors to facilitate the achievement of this object, it being clearly understood that nothing shall be done which may prejudice the civil and religious rights of existing non-Jewish communities in Palestine or the rights and political status enjoyed by Jews in any other country.

equal effort on his part to bring the cause of Zionism and the Jewish state to the forefront of British consciousness. To Weizmann, the Balfour Declaration was a huge step in the right direction. It also brought him one step closer to his future election as the president of the WZO in 1920 and, years later, as the first president of the new state of Israel.

The Palestinians, however, were not so sure they would be treated well by the declaration. Besides, they claimed, the Balfour Declaration was in direct conflict with another agreement made earlier during World War I. This agreement, called the Hussein-McMahon Correspondence, was made between the British, French, and Arabs in the Middle East. The Arabs believed this agreement said they would be guaranteed an independent kingdom after the war. This kingdom would span the entire area of Palestine. With the Balfour Declaration, this would be impossible. How could they control all of Palestine if the Jews built a nation there? The Balfour

Declaration, the Arabs said, was in direct contradiction to what they had been promised. There was no way it would work.

The Palestine Mandate

On July 24, 1922, the British government established the Palestine mandate, later known more commonly as the British mandate, at what became known as the San Remo Conference. The mandate officially separated Palestine into two parts, one on each side of the Jordan River. East of the river would be Arab

Throngs of Arab protesters fill the streets of Jaffa. One demonstrator in the background holds a sign that reads "Down with the Balfour Declaration."

Biography: Chaim Weizmann

Chaim Weizmann, a Russian-born scientist, was born in 1874. He went to school in Europe and before long joined the Zionist movement.

In 1905, Weizmann moved to Great Britain. There he became a member of the General Zionist Council. Years later, in 1918, Weizmann was elected to lead the Zionist Commission, a group sent to Palestine by the British to work toward the creation of a Jewish state in Palestine.

In 1920, Weizmann was elected president of the World Zionist Organization. He played a major role in the movement to partition Palestine into Jewish- and Palestinian-controlled areas. Then, in 1948, when his goals were finally met and Israel was declared an independent nation, he was elected to be the country's first president. Weizmann remained the president of Israel until he died in 1952.

territory. West of the river would belong to the Jews. This was all in accordance with the Balfour Declaration.

Part of the mandate text reads:

Whereas the Principal Allied Powers have also agreed that the Mandatory should be responsible for putting into effect the declaration originally made on November 2nd, 1917, by the Government of His Britannic Majesty, and adopted by the said Powers, in favour of the establishment in Palestine of a national home for the Jewish people, it being clearly understood that nothing should be done which might prejudice the civil and religious rights of existing non-Jewish communities in Palestine, or the rights and political status enjoyed by Jews in any other country; and Whereas recognition has thereby been given to the historical connection of the Jewish people with Palestine and to the grounds for reconstituting their national home in that country; and Whereas the Principal Allied Powers have selected His Britannic Majesty as the Mandatory for Palestine. . .

While most Jews were happy with the Palestine mandate, there were people on both sides of the conflict who claimed it was unfair.

For one, a smaller group within the Zionist movement called the World Union of Zionist Revisionists rejected the idea of partitioning Palestine altogether. They believed a Jewish state should be created on both sides of the Jordan River, not merely on one side. They felt that Jews had a right to the entire area and shouldn't have to leave any for the Palestinians. These revisionists completely opposed any Arab rule in Palestine. They called for the returning Diaspora Jews to stand up against the British and their mandate. (In 1937, the revisionists planned to do just that and created a military group called the Irgun Zvai Leumi (IZL). The Irgun's goal was to force the British to leave Palestine.)

Arabs, too, were unhappy with the mandate. They saw the mandate as a blatant move toward eliminating their right to a land they, too, believed was theirs. Arabs had been living on the land for nearly as long as the Jews. They felt the mandate unfairly favored the Jews, giving the Jewish population exactly what it wanted at the Palestinians' expense.

The mandate officially began in 1922. At the time, Britain was in sole control of Palestine. It was now Britain's responsibility to implement the partition plan and help the Jews create a nation in Palestine. Once that was accomplished, the British could leave.

British soldiers sent to keep the peace between Arabs and Jews come upon the body of an Arab boy killed during a terrorist bombing. It was soon learned that Irgun rebels planted the bomb.

The Jewish population, which was known as the Yishuv, took advantage of the mandate. With the British there to keep order, the Yishuv went about creating a new government. They created government committees and voted people into office. They also created the National Council to establish the basic foundations for a future nation.

Meanwhile, conflict in Palestine was on the rise. Arabs began rioting in protest of the growing Jewish presence. Attacks against the Jews became more and more common. Jews protested that the British were not fulfilling their mandate. They claimed the British were not doing enough to prevent these attacks.

The British did take one important step in response to the increasing violence. In 1939, the British handed down the so-called British White Paper. It called for the restriction of Jewish immigration to Palestine. The British hoped this would relieve the mounting tensions. Instead, it served to upset the Zionists. The Zionists, of course, believed that Jews from all over the world should be allowed to move to Palestine and settle. At this point in time, they were especially concerned that Jews be able to flee Nazi persecution in Europe and have a place to come and settle. They decided to completely reject the White Paper rules.

The British found themselves in trouble. Nothing they did seemed to make both sides happy. Tensions were rising. Living and working in the area were becoming dangerous.

CHAPTER 2

A CALL TO ARMS

Tensions between Arabs and Jews continued to rise in the region. More and more European Jews poured into Palestine. They fled war-torn Europe and Adolf Hitler's persecution. Any Jewish family with enough money escaped before they could be rounded up by the Nazis for shipment to concentration camps. Within a few years, by 1943, the Holocaust would find Nazis murdering Jews daily by the thousands.

Near the end of WWII, in 1945, Jewish leaders in Palestine knew of the Holocaust. They saw, now more than ever, that forming a Jewish state was important to Jewish freedom everywhere—to their very survival, in fact. Meanwhile, Palestinian and Arab aggression against such a state continued. Protests, riots, and terrorist attacks—coming from both sides—became common occurrences.

The British became increasingly frustrated with how difficult—impossible, really—it was to keep order in Palestine. Eventually they became so frustrated they decided they could no longer do their job. They decided to leave.

Prelude to War: The Mandate Ends

In the spring of 1947, Britain turned the problem over to the United Nations.

A column of British soldiers prepares to set off from the town of Tiberias, which borders the Sea of Galilee in Palestine.

The United Nations put together a committee to decide what to do next. The mandate would come to an end, and Palestine would be independent. Yet to be determined, though, was just how—and if—Palestine would be divided.

On November 29, 1947, the United Nations held a vote at its headquarters in New York City. The majority of those who voted felt that Palestine should be divided into two states: one Jewish and one Arab. They said the two states should be linked economically. Jerusalem was to be another major link between the two peoples but would not belong entirely to either state. Instead, Jerusalem would be an international city.

Some of those who voted disagreed with this division. They felt that Palestine should be a single state, not divided, with Jerusalem as its capital. Jews and Arabs could live in different areas, but they would all exist within one nation. The majority ruled, of course, and despite Arab protests, the United Nations went with the partition plan.

The transition period began with British troops and government officials leaving Palestine. The plan was that within two months of this evacuation, independent Arab and Jewish states would be established. One of the two parties— the Jews—was happy. They would finally have their own nation—Israel. The other side—the Arab Palestinians—were unhappy. Their worst fears were suddenly becoming reality.

The Palestinian Response: A Call to Arms

The situation quickly grew worse. Immediately after the resolution was declared, a group called the Arab Higher

United Nations Resolution 181 (II)
November 29, 1947

Future Government of Palestine

The General Assembly . . . Considers that the present situation in Palestine is one which is likely to impair the general welfare and friendly relations among nations;

Takes note of the declaration by the mandatory power that it plans to complete its evacuation of Palestine by 1 August 1948;

Recommends to the United Kingdom, as the mandatory power for Palestine, and to all other Members of the United Nations the adoption and implementation, with regard to the future government of Palestine, of the Plan of Partition with Economic Union set out below.

Independent Arab and Jewish States and the Special International Regime for the City of Jerusalem, set forth in part III of this plan, shall come into existence in Palestine two months after the evacuation of the armed forces of the mandatory Power has been completed but in any case not later than 1 October 1948. The boundaries of the Arab State, the Jewish State, and the City of Jerusalem shall be as described in parts II and III below.

The period between the adoption by the General Assembly of its recommendation on the question of Palestine and the establishment of the independence of the Arab and Jewish States shall be a transitional period.

Committee (AHC) stated that it was not acceptable. The AHC was the governmental organization of the Palestinians. It declared a strike. People began to riot all over Palestine. Arabs revolted in protest. Things were getting out of control. It appeared that war was on the way.

Meanwhile, the British police prepared to leave. And though the mandate was supposed to be in place for a short while longer, it was becoming more and more difficult to control the population. Deciding it wasn't worth it to get too involved in the growing unrest, the British essentially stood back and let things go. Their main goal was to evacuate Palestine as soon as possible. They set a date: May 15, 1948.

By January, the British retreat was fully underway. They left many major cities, including places like Tel Aviv and Jericho. When they left, they took with them the last chance of maintaining law and order. With the police gone, Jews and Arabs, who often lived side by side in the same towns and communities, fought at will. The riots continued, as the Palestinians refused to accept what was apparently coming their way: partition.

Moving Toward War

As tensions continued to build, both sides in the conflict prepared for war. The riots grew in size and number across Palestine. People and governments from inside and outside the region saw that the partition plan would not go into effect peacefully.

When the rioting began, those involved were mainly Palestinian Arabs. They were not well organized. They were merely groups of youths and other protestors set on making their voices heard. The Palestinians were certainly not prepared for war. They couldn't possibly wage a war against Israel on their own, and they knew it. They felt that they had to do something, though.

British troops attempt to quell a riot at the Jaffa Gate in Jerusalem. This angry outburst was part of a larger revolt against the British mandate.

What the Palestinians did have were their neighbors. Palestine was surrounded by Arab nations. Palestinian leaders hoped these nations would stand by their side in the event of war. Knowing this, the Arab Higher Committee attempted to keep the Palestinians under control as long as possible. Their goal was to round up military support from their neighbors before all-out war started. If they did not, the Palestinians—who had almost no military training—would be in serious trouble.

The AHC went to work. It established local divisions, or "national committees," in towns all over Palestine. These committees tried to keep order in the towns, but at the same time strove to bring in weapons, ammunition, and support from the surrounding Arab countries. But getting organized was not easy, and the AHC was ultimately not successful. The Palestinians had no central command and no true leadership to create a forceful army that could fight the Jewish population with any hope of success. As war drew closer, it looked more and more likely that the only hope for Palestinians would be through direct intervention by the Arab states.

Fortunately for the Palestinians, the Arab League had decided to support their struggle. The league saw military assistance as the best it could offer. The Arab League members thought the Jews were treating the Palestinians unfairly. By the summer of 1947, the Arab governments of the region had formed a plan for the approaching war.

The Yishuv was unsure how to deal with the approaching war. Should the Israeli army go on the offensive to repel

Biography: David Ben-Gurion

David Ben-Gurion was born in Poland on October 16, 1886. His family raised him according to the Hebrew religion and taught him the Zionist belief that Israel was the Promised Land for the Jewish people. Ben-Gurion was just a teenager when he decided to leave Poland to explore Zionism further. He moved to Palestine in 1906.

David Ben-Gurion

In Palestine, Ben-Gurion quickly found he fit right in with the active Zionist groups that were present there. A born leader, he was soon one of the top organizers of the Zionist movement. But Zionism was not appreciated by many in Palestine, and before long he was expelled from the region. He was told that his views were dangerous and controversial, and he was forced to leave.

Ben-Gurion moved to the United States. For three years, he lived in New York, continuing to gather support for Zionism and a Jewish homeland in Palestine. In 1918, after World War I, he returned to Palestine, which was then governed by Great Britain.

Back in Palestine, Ben-Gurion quickly rose to become the leader of the Zionist movement, and in 1948, with Chaim Weizmann as president, he was elected the first prime minister of Israel. On May 14, 1948, Ben-Gurion declared Israel's independence. It was this declaration that set in motion the brutal war that would last for the next year and a half.

Ben-Gurion would serve as Israel's prime minister for years to come, at one point resigning only to come back again a few years later. He grew to become one of Israel's greatest leaders. He died on December 1, 1973.

potential Arab invaders before they attacked? Or should the Israelis remain on the defensive and see what happened, while at the same time making efforts to keep the situation under control?

Prime Minister Ben-Gurion brought his advisers together to discuss what to do. There were arguments for both sides—both to attack and to wait it out. What was known for certain is that the Yishuv could no longer turn to the British to maintain law and order. Ultimately, this led to the decision to carry out strategic attacks against the Arabs whenever and wherever they were deemed to be threatening.

Gathering an Army

In the fall of 1947, that plan became even more concrete. The Arab League gathered in the city of Alia, Lebanon, to create a military committee. The committee focused on what to do militarily when the time came for war. An Iraqi general named Ismail Safwat led this committee. Safwat and the committee members concluded that the Arab nations needed well-trained troops to help the Palestinians. They also thought that the best chance for success would be if the war were short and decisive. The committee would have to put strong leaders in charge of the troops. It would also have to formulate a plan that would guarantee victory.

The committee nominated an Iraqi general named Taha al-Hashimi as inspector general of the Arab Liberation Army (ALA). It also appointed a man from Lebanon named Fawzi al-Qawukji to command the ALA in the field. These two men would be in charge of the army. It would be up to them to direct the troops in the war.

The ALA would be an all-Arab army. Trained troops from the surrounding Arab countries, as well as Palestinians and other Arab volunteers, would make up the fighting force. The Arab League would supply the army with all the gear, weapons, and ammunition it needed to win the war. But some within the Arab League disagreed as to how the war should be fought. On one side were those who thought

On October 2, 1947, Arab leaders met in Lake Success, New York, to prepare the case for Palestinian self-determination during a meeting at the United Nations. Shown here left to right are the delegates from Iraq, Saudi Arabia, and Egypt.

Palestinians should do all the fighting. This group wanted to simply give the Palestinians the equipment and money they needed to get the job done. On the other side were those who thought the Arab armies should be fully involved and committed, not just passive observers to the struggle.

These two groups began to work out the details. Meanwhile, the ALA began gathering troops from its member countries. Palestinians made up the majority of the troops. There were also Syrians, Lebanese, Iraqis, Egyptians, and others.

On January 10, 1948, the first ALA soldiers entered Palestine from Lebanon. A little more than a week later, more troops entered Palestine by crossing the Jordan River. The troops moved into the region and spread across the many villages to prepare for fighting. By the beginning of March, there were at least 10,000 Arab soldiers all over Palestine, including Jerusalem and other major cities. The war had yet to start, but the Arabs appeared to be ready.

But looks can be deceiving. In truth, the Arab Liberation Army was not well trained. Its equipment was old and outdated. Most of the soldiers had never even fought in battle. The training they had undergone was minimal. Moreover, the leadership was not well organized. Once in battle, the leadership would prove to be incompetent. But the mere presence of the ALA gave the Palestinians hope. They saw the Arab League forces as a sign that they were not alone in this struggle. They could now imagine victory, whereas before they had no chance at all.

Jewish Leaders React

Meanwhile, Ben-Gurion and his advisers reacted to the buildup of Arab soldiers in the region. They saw the armed Arab presence as a sure sign that war was not far away. The Jewish leaders were not certain when the battle would begin, but they knew it would come soon. As they made war plans of their own, they struggled to prevent the ALA from bringing weapons into Palestine. They trained soldiers and purchased arms. By April 1948, the Israeli troops, known as the Haganah, were ready for battle. They numbered nearly 20,000. But fighting wasn't their only job. The Haganah also worked to keep order on the streets of the many villages and cities.

While each side built on its military strength, chaos was the order of the day on the streets. Arabs were ambushing Jews as they traveled between cities. Jewish border settlements came under attack from ALA troops. Random shootings and riots became more common. Car bombs from those on both sides of the conflict killed dozens of people. Eventually, there was even fighting between the Jews and the British, as some Jews believed the British troops were ignoring their duty to keep order in Palestine. War had not yet begun, but conflict was spreading across all of Palestine, and it was getting worse by the day.

Civilians Caught in the Middle

By April 1948, the British evacuation of Palestine was in full order. The British, however, weren't the only ones on the run.

Also leaving the country were thousands of Palestinian civilians. Jewish civilians fled, too, but in smaller numbers. Civilians were fleeing from what they saw as an inevitable war. Most civilians wanted nothing to do with the fighting. They just wanted to get through the whole ordeal in one piece.

The Israeli leadership managed to talk most Jews into staying put. But the Palestinian leadership was not so lucky. Arab civilians recognized just how dangerous their homes had become. The Jewish Haganah was taking over many Arab villages and Arab areas. An attack by the Jewish group Irgun Zvai Leumi (IZL) resulted in more than 100 Palestinians killed in the town of Deir Yassin. Others feared they were next. Conditions were getting worse every day.

The economy was terrible. Jobs were scarce, and living supplies were dwindling. The future did not look bright. Many civilians did not think staying was worth the trouble or the danger. They began pouring out of the country any way they could. They piled into pickup trucks, walked on foot with donkeys in tow, or crammed into cars and buses. They fled by the thousands—estimates range as many as 300,000 total—out of Palestine and into the surrounding Arab countries.

The Final Push Toward War: Readying the Troops

As the Arabs were sending their troops into Palestine in anticipation of the declaration of Israeli statehood, the Yishuv, too, was preparing for battle. The Jews established a military draft in which young and healthy men capable of fighting were required to join the army. This army grew quickly. Training was intense. It was organized, well-equipped, and ready to fight.

Meanwhile, in a last-ditch effort to prevent war, diplomatic talks were underway between the two sides. England, the United States, the United Nations, and even the International Red Cross all took part in the talks. Their goal was to help the Palestinians and Israelis come to a truce. They would not succeed.

With their backs to the Mediterranean Sea, Jewish Defense Force troops train for battle in trenches in March 1948. Preparations for war were stepped up as the British began departing from Palestine.

The Eve of War

With the war just days away, it appeared as though the Arab coalition of armies would have its way with the Israelis. After all, how could a half-dozen countries intent on destroying one tiny, brand-new nation fail to win? It would be quick and easy, a stroll through the park. The Israelis didn't stand a chance.

But looks were deceiving. Despite the fact that Israel had yet to be recognized as a nation, that it was small and

Lebanese soldiers of the Arab Liberation Army man French-made 2.9 inch (75-millimeter) mortars in Jersulam in May 1948. They were part of a heavy weapons group mobilized for skirmishes against Israeli forces.

surrounded by countries that hoped to gobble it up, it was no weakling. In fact, it was more than adequately prepared to defend its soon-to-be-established borders. For one, the Israeli forces were led by thousands of battle-tested soldiers who had fought bravely in World War II just a few years earlier. They knew exactly what they were doing when it came to war. Their battle experience was far superior to that of the Arabs, and they knew the terrain. This was their land. They had the resources to defend it, including tanks, fighter jets, and plenty of guns and ammunition, and they were ready to do whatever it took. They were also well organized. Israel's army was no group of amateurs. On the contrary, this was a team of professionals. Whoever came knocking on their door had better be ready to fight.

The Arabs, on the other hand, lacked the leadership or the experience to pull the war off. Their soldiers were poorly trained, and most had never seen battle before. There was no telling what would happen once the bullets started to fly. They had the numbers—thousands more troops than the Israelis—but they didn't have the know-how or the resources to put those numbers to work. They prepared to invade, but they had no idea what a disaster they were in for.

CHAPTER 3

THE ARAB INVASION

On May 14, 1948, the British mandate came to an end. Israeli leader David Ben-Gurion read the Jewish Declaration of Independence, and the State of Israel was born. Israel was now an independent country.

In addition, restrictions on Jewish immigration, which had been created with the 1939 British White Paper, were now lifted. Jews from all over the world could now immigrate freely to Israel to start a new life.

But the Arab states were not happy. They had vowed to do all they could to prevent the establishment of a Jewish state and to ensure that all of Palestine would be in Arab hands. The time to fight had come. The first Arab-Israeli War—Egypt, Syria, Transjordan (present-day Jordan), Iraq, Lebanon, and the Arab Palestinians against Israel—was about to begin.

The Arabs Invade Palestine

The Arab armies invaded Palestine on May 15, 1948. Armies from Lebanon, Syria, Transjordan, Iraq, and Egypt all joined in the onslaught. They attacked from the north, east, and south. The major fighting began with an Egyptian air raid on Tel Aviv. From there it continued to spread to major cities throughout Israel, including

Surrounded by various ministers of his new government, Israeli prime minister David Ben-Gurion reads the Jewish Declaration of Independence, making official the founding of Israel on May 14, 1948.

Ramallah, Nablus, and even Jerusalem. The Arab attackers were well equipped at the start of the invasion. They drove in on tanks and armored personnel carriers. They carried machine guns and mortars. They had truckloads of ammunition.

This was also the first day of Israeli independence. The civil unrest had been reshaped into a true war. The real fighting had begun.

From the start, the goal of the Arab army was to prevent Palestine from coming under complete control of the Israelis. The Arabs feared this might happen if they stood back and did nothing. They worried that the Israeli army would take land that had been promised to the Palestinians in the partition agreement. They also worried that Palestinians would be hopeless without their support. This hopelessness would translate into even more refugees fleeing into the surrounding Arab countries.

As the battles commenced, the Arabs appeared to be at an advantage. They had more troops than did the Israelis. They had more guns and ammunition. It didn't look good for the Israelis. When it came to manpower, guns, and ammunition, they were far overpowered. They had little in terms of firepower because the British mandate restricted them from building an army.

At first, the Israelis suffered severe losses. Places such as Mishmar Hayarden to the north fell to the Arabs. To the south, Yad Mordehai was lost. The Arabs pushed inward, and the Israelis could do relatively little to halt their movements.

But soon, the tide turned. Thanks to the superior Israeli war experience and thanks to a renewed flow of ammunition and weapons into the newly formed state, within a few weeks they were building their army and they had stopped the Arabs in their tracks. They were even able to turn the war momentum in their direction. The Israelis, still outnumbered, went on the attack. They had no other choice. It was fight or die.

The Battles for Degania A and B

One of the major victories for Israel came against the Syrian army, which attacked two Israeli kibbutzes, or villages, known as Degania A and Degania B. The Syrian assault on Degania A began on May 20. The Syrians' goal was to take control of bridges that crossed the Jordan River. The Syrians blasted the Israelis with their tanks and mortars as their soldiers advanced. They had far superior manpower, and it appeared to be a hopeless situation for the few Israelis who were defending their position. Somehow, though, the Israelis managed to fight back—just enough to turn the Syrians away.

Next came Degania B. Again, the Israelis successfully defended their home. Intense shelling by the Syrians did little to weaken the Israeli fighters. Surprised by how strong the Israelis were, the Syrians turned and fled.

Similar battles took place throughout the war, and despite the odds, the Israelis were able to turn back the aggressors time and time again.

The Israelis had anticipated a large-scale attack and had prepared their army for the worst. They were surprised, then, when they were able to repel the Arab forces. The Israeli forces held off the attacks until the Arab army slowly ran out of supplies. It seemed the Arab forces had bitten off more than they could chew. Their massive invasion of Palestine was not going as planned.

Truce 1: June 11, 1948

Both sides had fought as hard as they could for nearly a month. Hundreds of soldiers had died on both sides of the battle lines.

Unfortunately for the Arab army, their invasion did not result in the quick and decisive victory they had hoped for. Even worse, Palestinians continued to flee and the refugee situation was quickly becoming a crisis. In addition, the battles were taking their toll. Troops from both sides were exhausted. They were running out of energy.

On June 11, 1948, the United Nations stepped in. A truce was declared—a time-out from the war. The truce was scheduled to last for four weeks. During that time there would be no fighting and no troop movements. The two sides were to rest, tend to their injured, resupply, and hopefully work out a compromise before the end of the four weeks.

Of course, the truce didn't go exactly as planned. Both sides did move troops to more strategic locations. Shootings did occur. And while some important Arab leaders called for negotiations that could have potentially resulted in a treaty, there was little hope of an agreement this early in the fighting. For the most part, neither side seemed willing to budge.

The Israelis used the truce to their advantage. They quickly stocked up on things like airplanes and weapons. They brought more troops in for the fighting. They would be more than prepared for the next round of the war. They would go on the offensive this time, not the other way around.

Ten-Day Campaign

On July 9, 1948, the fighting resumed. This time the battles would be known as the Ten-Day Campaign, lasting ten days

Happy Jewish children in Tel Aviv mob an Australian soldier serving with the United Nations during a lull in the fighting. The UN moderated two cease-fires during the conflict.

before coming to a close on July 19 with the second truce. During the campaign, the Jewish forces were able to gain significant amounts of land from the Arabs. They took over three Arab cities and more than 100 smaller villages. Meanwhile, more and more Palestinians fled the country in fear of their lives. The surrounding Arab nations were being flooded with Palestinian refugees. The Arabs were losing the war.

Still, despite the Israeli gains, the Arab army refused to give up. When the UN declared the second truce on July 19,

Onlookers gawk as an armored vehicle of the Israeli forces drives down Ben Yehuda Street in Jerusalem during the second truce that began in July 1948. The break in the fighting allowed both sides breathing room to plan more attacks.

both sides were still fighting. Once again, both sides would use the time-out to resupply and prepare for more. The UN monitored the second truce. The calm in the middle of the storm enabled both sides to prepare for more fighting.

The Israel Defense Force (IDF) focused its attention on organizing a potential offensive against the Egyptian army. The Egyptians were threatening to the south. The IDF moved arms and ammunition into position on the front lines. Ben-Gurion had finally come to the realization that the only way Israel would get out of this mess was to turn the direction of the war around. It would now be the attacker instead of being attacked itself.

The Arabs also worked to bring reinforcements into Palestine. But now their main issue was not maintaining the offensive, which they could no longer do anyway thanks to decreased strength, but to prepare for a defensive stand. They saw that the tide of the war was turning, and they realized that all they could do now was try to prevent a successful Israeli counterattack.

The truce lasted two months. During that time there were many political meetings between Israeli leaders and individual leaders of the surrounding Arab countries. Egypt, Transjordan, and Lebanon all worked with Israel individually to establish peace along their shared borders and, through political negotiations, to regain the lands they had lost in fighting. Iraq worked for a solution as well. Meanwhile, the Palestinian situation was not good. The Palestinians had hoped that the Arab coalition would come in and prevent the establishment of the State of

The Israel-Syria Armistice Agreement: Article I

With a view to promoting the return of permanent peace in Palestine and in recognition of the importance in this regard of mutual assurances concerning the future military operations of the Parties, the following principles, which shall be fully observed by both Parties during the armistice, are hereby affirmed:

1. The injunction of the Security Council against resort to military force in the settlement of the Palestine question shall henceforth be scrupulously respected by both Parties. The establishment of an armistice between their armed forces is accepted as an indispensable step toward the liquidation of armed conflict and the restoration of peace in Palestine.

2. No aggressive action by the armed forces—land, sea or air—of either Party shall be undertaken, planned or threatened against the people or the armed forces of the other; it being understood that the use of the term "planned" in this context has no bearing on normal staff planning as generally practised in military organisations.

3. The right of each Party to its security and freedom from fear of attack by the armed forces of the other shall be fully respected.

Israel. That was now obviously impossible. The Palestinian dilemma was worse now than when the war began.

July 20, 1949: The Israel-Syria Armistice Agreement Ends the War

On July 20, 1949, Syria and Israel came to an official peace agreement. This agreement was the beginning of the end of Israel's War for Independence.

The fighting was finally over. Unfortunately, the larger problems of the region—including land issues, political issues, and cultural issues—were far from fixed. The Arab-Israeli conflict was nowhere close to being resolved.

A group called the Palestine Conciliation Commission was given the task of ensuring that peace would last in the area. Talks were held between all parties involved, including the Israelis, the Palestinians, and the surrounding Arab nations. The goal was to find a permanent solution to the conflict. But progress was difficult. Some might say it was, and is, impossible.

CHAPTER 4

AFTER THE WAR: PROGRESS AND PROBLEMS

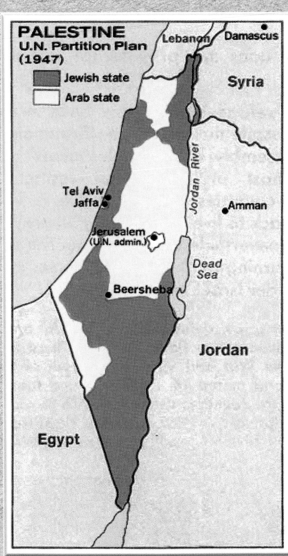

PALESTINE
U.N. Partition Plan
(1947)

Jewish state
Arab state

Lebanon
Damascus
Syria
Jordan River
Tel Aviv
Jaffa
Amman
Jerusalem
(U.N. admin.)
Dead
Sea
Beersheba
Jordan
Egypt

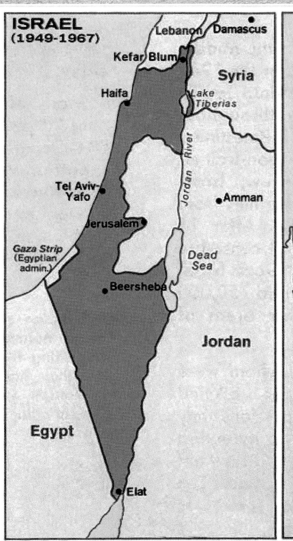

ISRAEL
(1949-1967)

Lebanon
Damascus
Kefar Blum
Syria
Haifa
Lake
Tiberias
Tel Aviv-
Yafo
Jordan River
Amman
Jerusalem
Gaza Strip
(Egyptian
admin.)
Dead
Sea
Beersheba
Jordan
Egypt
Elat

When the fighting came to an end, Israel had clearly emerged as the winner. Not only had this brand-new country fended off the Arab invaders, but it had also managed to gain control of much of the land that had been originally destined for a new Palestinian state. The Palestinians and neighboring Arabs had started the war because they were unhappy with the partition plan. Now they had even less land than they would have had had they accepted the plan in the first place.

Now, with the war over, it was time to reestablish borders and determine what land belonged to which countries. Various agreements drew out so-called demilitarized zones between Israel and Egypt, Syria, and Jordan. These were neutral areas between countries that could not be occupied militarily. It was a way of preventing conflict from erupting between opposing armies.

The land that remained for the Palestinian state was divided between Jordan and Egypt. Jordan took the West Bank into its kingdom. Egypt took the Gaza Strip. Jerusalem, which had been designated as a neutral international city by the partition plan, was now divided. The western part of the city would belong to Israel, while the eastern side would belong to Jordan.

ISRAEL and Occupied Territory (June 10, 1967–1979)

These three maps depict from left to right the shift in territories in Palestine from 1947 to 1967. Successive wars have yielded the Israelis de facto control over all of Palestine.

Behind the Scenes of War

Even as the war raged on, Israel began to do the things any new nation would do: focus on building a democracy, working on international relations, and creating an effective government. In February 1949, Chaim Weizmann was elected the first president of Israel and David Ben-Gurion was chosen to be the prime minister. A few months later, Israel became an official member of the United Nations. Countries from all over the world now recognized Israel as an independent state. Meanwhile, more and more Jews immigrated to Israel. The country was growing not only in numbers but also in reputation.

In addition to the land issues, there remained the problem of refugees. The surrounding Arab nations declared that the refugees who had flooded across their borders must be allowed to return to their homes. This would become an issue that continues to dominate the Arab-Israeli conflict even today.

The years immediately following the war were characterized by continued Arab opposition to Israeli statehood. Arab nations continued to stand prepared for further fighting, as they feared Israel could attempt to take land from across their borders at any time. They also continued to protest what they saw as the loss of Palestinian rights in Israel. They felt that Palestinians were still treated unfairly, as outcasts not allowed to return to their homeland.

Much as they did before Israel's War for Independence, tensions picked up again. Before long, armed confrontations

One of the unfortunate legacies of the conflicts between the Palestinians and the Israelis is the refugee situation. The Baka'a Refugee Camp in Jordan is one of many bordering Israeli-occupied territories. Generations of Palestinians have lived in such camps, most of them in abject poverty. They are a people without a country.

The Six-Day War

In 1967, during what became known as the Six-Day War, the Israeli-Arab conflict took yet another turn. This war resulted in Israel occupying the West Bank and Gaza Strip, which had been controlled by Jordan and Egypt since the end of the War of Independence. The Palestinians who lived there would now live under Israeli rule. Israel also took full control of Jerusalem. This would be the source of bitter disagreement—and much fighting—for years to come.

between Arabs and Israelis were the norm once again. Thousands of small fights between the two sides took place in the early 1950s. Soon, war—in fact, a series of wars—was on the way again.

Unresolved Issues

Today there are many reasons why the Israeli-Palestinian conflict continues, as shown in the newspaper headlines near the beginning of this book. The main reason for the fighting is the same as always: Two cultures, two distinct groups of people, feel they each have full right to the same small piece of land. Many of these people now understand that the only way to a solution is through peaceful negotiations and compromise. They see there is no way for everyone to be entirely happy, so both sides must show a willingness to give a little.

But a significant number of people are too upset with history to give in that easily. Many Palestinians, for instance, feel they have been wronged from the start. They point to the 1917 Balfour Declaration and say that their rights have never been honored as they should have been according to that law. Others point to the partition plan. They say Israel should return to the Palestinians all the land it took during the War for Independence and later wars. Still others think Israel has no right to exist whatsoever.

Another problem is that of the Palestinian refugees—the men, women, and children who were either forced

An Israeli soldier at the Ares checkpoint scans the identifying documents of a Palestinian man coming into Israel from the Gaza Strip. Such checkpoints can often take many hours to navigate and can become the focal points for violence.

from their homes because of war or takeovers by the Israelis or those who left voluntarily in anticipation of the dangers of war that were approaching. These refugees have no permanent place to settle. Many wish to return to their homes in Israel, but they are not allowed to do so.

The future of Israel, the Palestinians, and the Arab world that surrounds them depends on willingness by all sides to negotiate and compromise. Otherwise, there is little hope for a solution, and the fighting will go on.

Al-Nakba The Arabic word for Israel's War of Independence, meaning "the Catastrophe."

Arab League An international organization founded in 1945 made up of Arab countries.

Balfour Declaration A declaration issued by the British government in 1917 that expressed the intent of Britain to work toward the creation of a Jewish national home in Palestine.

Diaspora The settling of Jews outside of Palestine after they were forced to leave by the Babylonians.

Haganah A Jewish military organization.

Irgun A military group created in 1937 by the World Union of Zionist Revisionists to oppose the British mandate created in 1922.

Israelites Members of an ancient nation that once existed in Palestine.

Palestine An ancient region in southwest Asia that extends east from the Mediterranean Sea.

Palestine mandate A law issued by the British that officially divided Palestine into Arab and Jewish territories; known today as the British Mandate.

partition To divide into parts.

refugee A person who flees his or her home or country in order to escape danger.

White Paper A 1937 British publication that called for the restriction of Jewish immigration to British-controlled Palestine.

World Zionist Organization An organization created
in 1897 with the purpose of establishing a national
home for the Jewish people in Palestine.

Zionism An international movement whose original goal
was to establish a Jewish religious community in
Palestine and that now strives to gain support for
modern Israel.

Organizations

The Middle East Institute
1761 N Street NW
Washington, DC 20036-2882
(202) 785-1141
Web site: http://www.mideasti.org

Americans for Middle East Understanding
475 Riverside Drive, Room 245
New York, NY 10115-0245
(212) 870-2053
Web site: http://www.ameu.org

American Task Force on Palestine
815 Connecticut Avenue NW, Suite 1200
Washington, DC 20006
(202) 887-0177
Web site: http://www.americantaskforce.org

Web Sites

Due to the changing nature of Internet links, the Rosen Publishing Group, Inc., has developed an online list of Web sites related to the subjects of this book. This site is updated regularly. Please use this link to access the list:

http://www.rosenlinks.com/wcme/iswi

Gottfried, Ted. *The Israelis and Palestinians: Small Steps to Peace*. Brookfield, CT: Millbrook Press, 2000.

Harris, Nathaniel. *Israel and the Arab Nations in Conflict*. New York: Raintree/Steck Vaughn, 1999.

Long, Cathryn. *The Middle East in Search of Peace*. Brookfield, CT: Millbrook Press, 1996.

McAleavy, Tony. *The Arab-Israeli Conflict*. New York: SIGS Books and Multimedia, 1998.

Patterson, Jose. *Israel* (Country Fact Files). New York: Raintree/Steck Vaughn, 1997.

Smith, Debbie. *Israel: The Land*. New York: Crabtree Publishing, 1998.

BIBLIOGRAPHY

Gelber, Yoav. *Palestine 1948: War, Escape, and the Emergence of the Palestinian Refugee Problem.* Portland, OR: Sussex Academic Press, 2001.

Lorch, Netanel. *The Edge of the Sword: Israel's War of Independence, 1947–1949.* New York: G. P. Putnam's Sons, 1961.

Lustick, Ian, ed. *Arab-Israeli Relations: A Collection of Contending Perspectives and Recent Research*, Vol. 2. New York: Garland Publishing, Inc., 1994.

Reich, Bernard, and Gershon Kieval. *Israel: Land of Tradition and Conflict.* Boulder, CO: Westview Press, Inc., 1993.

INDEX

A

Arab Higher Committee (AHC), 26–27, 30
Arab-Israeli War, 41–49
Arab League, 30, 32, 33, 34
Arab Liberation Army (ALA), 32, 33, 34

B

Babylonians, 13
Balfour Declaration, 17, 18–19, 20
Ben-Gurion, David, 17, 31, 32, 35, 41, 47, 52
Britain/British, 17, 18, 21, 22, 23, 25, 28, 31, 35
British/Palestine mandate, 19–23, 26, 41, 42
British White Paper, 23, 41

D

Degania A and B, 43
Diaspora, 13, 14, 21

E

Egypt/Egyptians, 10, 34, 41, 47, 51, 54
Europe, 14, 15, 20, 23, 25

G

Gaza Strip, 5, 10, 51, 54
General Zionist Council, 20

H

Haganah, 35, 36
Hashimi, Taha al-, 32–33
Herzl, Theodor, 15–17

Hitler, Adolf, 25
Hussein-McMahon Correspondence, 18

I

Iraq/Iraqis, 4, 13, 34, 41
Irgun Zvai Leumi (IZL), 21, 36
Islam/Muslims, 9, 10, 14
Israel
    Arabs in, 42–43
    establishment of State of, 17, 18, 26, 41, 47–48
    geography of, 9
    history of, 10–13
Israel Defense Force (IDF), 47
Israel-Syria Armistice Agreement, 48

J

Jerusalem, 4, 10, 13, 26, 27, 42, 51, 54
Jewish Legion, 17
Jews/Judaism, 9, 10, 13, 14, 15, 17, 18, 20, 21, 22, 23, 25 26, 47, 28, 31, 35, 36–37, 41, 46, 52
Jordan/Transjordan, 9, 41, 47, 51

L

Lebanon, 4, 32, 41, 47

M

Middle East, 4, 5, 6, 9, 18
    Arab rule of, 13–14, 18–19

N

National Council, 23
Nazis, 23, 25

O

Ottoman Turks, 14

P

Palestine/Palestinians
Arabs in, 21–22, 23, 27, 30, 32, 34, 35, 36, 41, 44, 47
Britain and, 21, 23, 25, 26, 28, 31, 32, 35
geography of, 9–10
partition of, 19–21, 22, 26, 55
Palestine Conciliation Commission, 49

Q

Qawukji, Fawzi al-, 32–33

S

Safwat, Ismail, 32
San Remo Conference, 19
Six-Day War, 54
Syria/Syrians, 34, 41, 43, 51

T

Ten-Day Campaign, 45–46

U

United Nations, 25–26, 37, 44, 46, 47, 52
Resolution 181 (II) of, 27
United States, 4, 31, 37

W

Weizmann, Chaim, 17–18, 20, 31, 52
West Bank, 10, 51, 54
World Union of Zionist Revisionists, 21
World War I, 14, 17, 18, 31
World War II, 25, 39
World Zionist Congress, 15, 17
World Zionist Organization, 17, 18, 20

Y

Yishuv, 23, 30, 32, 36

Z

Zionism/Zionists, 15–17, 18, 20, 21, 23, 31
Zionist Commission, 20

About the Author

Chris Hayhurst is a freelance writer from Colorado.

Photo Credits